For Beginners

Beginner's Guide to Cycling Gear, Tips and Routes So You Can Ride Safely and Easily for Fitness and Fun

By Francis Cantrell

© **Copyright 2020 - All rights reserved.**

The content contained within this book may not be reproduced, duplicated or transmitted without direct written permission from the author or the publisher.

Under no circumstances will any blame or legal responsibility be held against the publisher or author for any damages, reparation, or monetary loss due to the information contained within this book. Either directly or indirectly.

Legal Notice:

This book is copyright protected. This book is only for personal use. You cannot amend, distribute, sell, use, quote or paraphrase any part, or the content within this book, without the consent of the author or publisher.

Disclaimer Notice:

Please note the information contained within this document is for educational and entertainment purposes only. All effort has been executed to present accurate, up to date and reliable, complete information. No warranties of any kind are declared or implied. Readers acknowledge that the author is not engaging in the rendering of legal, financial, medical or professional advice. The content within this book has been derived from various sources. Please consult a licensed professional before attempting any techniques outlined in this book.

By reading this document, the reader agrees that under no

circumstances is the author responsible for any losses, direct or indirect, which are incurred as a result of the use of information contained within this document, including, but not limited to, —errors, omissions, or inaccuracies.

Contents

Getting Started With Cycling 1

What You Need For Biking 4

Bike Types 8

Bike Seats and Comfort Bikes 11

Accessories Make All the Difference 14

Cargo Bags and Cycling Trailers 17

Competitive Biking 20

Cycling Can Involve the Family 23

Biking is Excellent for Getting in Shape 26

Biking for Health 29

Biking to Improve Cardio 32

Best Cycling Cities 36

Excellent Bike Trails 39

Cycling to Work 42

Travel Trips 45

Cycling Events 48

Organized Bike Rides 51

The Biking Getaway 54

There are Options for All Ages 57

The Health Advantages of Biking 60

The Ecological Advantages of Biking 63

Thank you for buying this book and I hope that you will find it useful. If you will want to share your thoughts on this book, you can do so by leaving a review on the Amazon page, it helps me out a lot.

Getting Started With Cycling

There are lots of methods to work out. These vary from walking, swimming, running, to lifting weights, or an assortment of other alternatives. You might work out with any of these. While each delivers results when approached intensely, one kind of workout might be included in the list. Numerous people might consider it as an enjoyable activity, however, it really includes working out. Plus, it is a method to include inter-generations. It ought to be obvious. It's cycling. And, yes, you might work out forever with this sport.

If you approach the sport as a long-lasting experience, you have actually taken a fantastic leap in numerous favorable directions. One benefit is the fact that you might bike solo, with a member of the family of any age, with buddies or perhaps competitively. Additionally, there are opportunities to bike for a great cause. In doing this, you might raise money for that cause, therefore assisting yourself and another person simultaneously.

It's a sport that you might delight in for your whole lifetime. However, this sport approached through regular exercise might quite possibly extend your life, and in this way, make your life much healthier. Who would not wish to shed pounds while seeing the world simultaneously, even if that world were your own community? Biking, as a sport, has actually grown greatly in the last decade. And, thanks to stationary bicycles, based upon where you live, is a year-round activity. When the weather condition is shabby, your bike might be that friendly one-wheeler in basement or the family room. It might not take you around the block, however, when it's 32 degrees or beneath, it's a quite good seat for seeing the world pass.

In fact, stationary bicycles have a number of benefits for the individual who insists upon taking up more than one task at the same time. If you can chew up and walk simultaneously, odds are good that you can ride a stationary bicycle and go through a book simultaneously, or maybe, see your favorite film while cycling in your basement. Attempt that while running, swimming or sky diving. You can't do it.

However, as you ride your bike off into the sundown, it's a sensation you would not trade for all the weight-lifting medals on the planet. And the very best part is that you might cycle forever regardless of your age or condition of that gizmo with 2 wheels, a handlebar, one chain, and a seat.

What You Need For Biking

When you ride your bike, you ought to think about tools and garments that are going to bring you convenience, and, likewise, keep you safe. Think about where you are going to be riding. What terrain are you going to be cycling through and what is the environment like? Make certain to check the weather condition prior to leaving and take the suitable clothing. Beneath are some products to take note of so as to make your trip more satisfying.

When you purchase a helmet, make certain that it is authorized by the Consumer Product Safety Commission (CPSC). Everybody's head is formed in a different way so try out various helmets up until you discover one that is comfortable. Adjust the helmet level on your head and change buckles and straps for an appropriate fit. When you are done changing your helmet, shake your head to ensure that it does not bounce around. It is among the most essential products that you can buy and the objective is to shield your head, and consequently, avoid brain injury.

Some things you should consider are:

Socks

Gloves

Bike shorts

Jacket

Jerseys

Shoes

When buying rain equipment, ensure you understand the distinction in between waterproof and water-resistant. To be water-resistant it should be made from water-resistant material and the joints need to be sealed. Waterproof is made from a component that fends off water, and is not water-resistant. Simply understand that there is a big difference.

You ought to constantly have an emergency situation bike set. Purchase a little bag that can hook beneath your bike seat. In this bag, you ought to include:

Tire levers

C02 Tire inflater

Extra tube

Water bottle to remain hydrated

Swiss Army knife

Consuming ample water is essential to lots of parts of your body, consisting of cells, brain, muscle & joints, heart, kidneys, skin, gastrointestinal system and preserving your temperature level. Even the tiniest loss of fluid can impact your focus and hinder your decision-making procedure. Without ample water, your body might end up being overheated and you might not have the ability to sweat.

Fundamental First Aid:

Antibiotic ointment

Non reusable gloves

Adhesive bandages

Sterile dressings

If you have unique requirements like diabetes, ensure you have your glucose display with you and some treats. Follow these easy suggestions, and you too can delight in biking for life!

Bike Types

There are lots of kinds of bikes to pick from. Which you pick ought to depend upon where you are going to be riding and what your goal is going to be. Some questions to pose are:

Am I riding for enjoyment?

Am I going to be riding for a workout?

Am I going to wish to go off the roadway?

Just how much do I wish to spend?

There are touring bikes, mountain bikes, utility bikes and recumbent bicycles, among others. Individuals ride bikes for numerous reasons. They might utilize their bike as transport or just for fun. They can likewise be utilized as a workout tool and for sport. Touring bikes are created for long journeys and have the capability to carry your individual possessions and other equipment. These kinds of bikes are appropriate for riding around the countryside and delighting in the view.

Mtb are created to be utilized off the road and have tough, long-lasting frames and wide-gauge tires. Suspension systems like air shocks or gas shocks are included for rough surfaces.

Recumbent Bikes are developed to make the most of comfort and reduce resistance. It might be hard to get accustomed to being horizontal, however, if you have any injuries that might stop you from cycling, then you might wish to check this type out.

Tandem bikes could be utilized for those who have some physical difficulties. Some considerations are to make certain the bike fits both individuals. This is going to assist to avoid injuries. A crucial thing to bear in mind is that there can just be a single captain.

Downhill biking is normally performed on a high surface. It might not be for everybody.

BMX bikes are created for stunts, tricks and racing on hilly dirt. There are contests that you can go into and even cash to be won.

Single track is a type of mountain cycling that is carried out on really narrow routes that could be narrow and steep with sharp turns and other challenges. This kind of riding takes a great deal of upper body strength.

There are bikes that can be used by even the youngest family member by connecting a tinier two-wheeled bike to the end of a bike.

Ice cycling is when individuals ride through snow and ice. It might not be for everybody due to the fact that it is more tiring.

Bike Seats and Comfort Bikes

For numerous people who like biking, riding their bikes could be a frustrating experience. While bike seats are developed for optimum effectiveness and convenience, they are not comfy for everybody. Numerous riders experience pain while riding. The shape of the seat can trigger discomfort or soreness.

Thankfully, there are a variety of alternatives for those who like to ride, however, who do not enjoy standard bike seats. Initially, numerous recumbent bikes have a different kind of seat. If you do not mind how you need to sit and ride with this kind of bike, it is a fantastic alternative.

There are likewise other kinds of convenience bikes that work splendidly. Furthermore, there are unique bike seats produced for individuals who are made uncomfortable by conventional bike seats. There are a couple of styles that make riding simple while keeping convenience in mind. If conventional bike seats make you uneasy, do not fret. You do not need to quit riding due to the pain. It is necessary to continue biking and enhancing your health, life and the environment. With a brand-new bike or bike seat, you are going to have the ability to ride like you enjoy. Whether you ride to work or simply ride sometimes for enjoyment, it is essential that you are comfy while you are riding.

If you are going to buy a brand-new bike or a brand-new seat, make sure to completely check all of your choices prior to deciding. While comfort seats and comfort bikes are developed specifically for individuals who are made uncomfortable by conventional bike seats, not all designs are best for everybody. Make certain the one you select is best for you. The salesmen at your neighborhood bike store ought to be more than pleased to make suggestions and to assist you in selecting.

They ought to likewise entirely support you in checking out all of your choices. Lots of convenience bikes are somewhat more pricey than routine bikes, however, that is not constantly the case. Depending upon the design and model you desire, comfort bike seats can vary in price from really low-cost to reasonably pricey. Obviously, you ought to make certain to get the bike or bike seat that makes you feel most comfy, so you can get the most out of your experiences.

Accessories Make All the Difference

A fantastic method to make cycling simpler is with cycling add-ons. There are a variety of choices when it concerns cycling accessories, and much of your decision is going to be based upon what you prefer. Nevertheless, there are a couple of accessories that almost every bicycle rider requires to make biking simpler.

A few of the most crucial cycling add-ons for cyclists to have are lights. In case you are ever going to bike when it is darker, or becoming dark, you need to have lights. Depending upon the time of year, it might be dark in the early morning and even late afternoon. If you bike to work or for another reason throughout these times, lights are important. Even if you do not intend to bike when it is dark, you ought to have lights simply in case. A strong light is ideal for the front of your bike, and a blinking light is finest for the rear of your bike. You might likewise wish to think about reflective clothes if you are going to be riding during the night.

Another extremely crucial bike accessory is a helmet. Helmets are not needed in certain states, however, they are an excellent option. While you might be a safe rider, it is ideal to prepare for contingencies. A helmet is going to assist secure your head in case of an incident, regardless of the severity. Lives have actually been protected by bike helmets. Besides, there are some comfy, contemporary and elegant styles offered.

A tire pump is another fantastic bike accessory to have. On the occasion that your bike tires ever require a little bit of air, your tire pump is going to be a lifesaver. While it is simple enough to take your bike to a gasoline station to utilize the air device, a tire pump in the house is going to spare you money and time. You ought to fill your tires with an air machine regularly anyhow, however, it is good to have a tire pump around if you require it.

Speedometers are an excellent add-on to have. Numerous are simple to use, and they can inform you how quickly you are riding, and typically how far you have actually gone. Speedometers are enjoyable to utilize.

Cargo Bags and Cycling Trailers

Those thinking about biking do a great deal for themselves and everybody else. Health enhances, and they lead by example. As a matter of fact, cycling has actually ended up being so prominent that much-needed and easy to use and devices are emerging everywhere.

While they have actually been around for a while, cargo bags and bike trailers make biking simpler. In case you have numerous things to bring with you, however, you still wish to bike, that is no longer inconceivable. Fortunately, it is simpler than ever to bike with extra valuables. Whether you wish to bike to the supermarket and require a location for your grocery bags, or wish to bike to an outdoor camping location and require room for your camping tent and more, freight bags and cycling trailers are simply what you require. Cycling trailers include a range of choices.

Typically, all the cycling trailers seen were for children. Cycling lovers might buckle their kids in, and tow them behind their bike. Those are, obviously, still offered, and much enhanced. Nevertheless, there are other cycling trailers out there today also. Along with the conventional kid trailers, there are trailers for other things too. These are excellent for long trips where you need to take the baggage of some kind, or perhaps for grocery shopping. The opportunities are unlimited.

Cargo bags are a tinier and less apparent choice than cycling trailers. These are perfect for a rider who typically deals with how ideally to take possessions with them on a trip. These bags are the ideal location to place a laptop computer, brief-case, and clothing if you ride to work. Likewise, they are best for reasonably little trips to the supermarket. If you are taking an over night outdoor camping journey, cargo bags can normally hold a little tent and some fundamental materials.

How you pick to utilize your cargo bags and cycling trailer to make biking simpler is your decision. The choices are endless, and you need to make certain to discover something that works for you which you take pleasure in utilizing.

Competitive Biking

You most likely feel as if you see more bicyclists out on the road nowadays. Not just are individuals relying on biking for much better health, however, they are relying on it as the supreme rush. Lots of people have actually seen biking as a competitive sport and have actually profited while doing so. No one ever used to consider biking as a legally competitive kind of sport, however, this is how it is now. It can begin with something basic like simply one race.

What's drawn a great deal of individuals in is that lots of charity and non-profit groups began sponsoring biking occasions to assist to raise money for their given causes. This pulls at the heartstrings of many individuals and they wish to do whatever they can to assist. This is where the turning point comes in because as soon as someone starts with biking, especially when it's for an excellent cause, they're connected! There are numerous excellent advantages to biking and when you pair it with the possibility of assisting an excellent cause, it's a no-brainer.

Those who sign on to take part in a biking charity race have no concept of how extensive the training could be. To be able to get involved successfully in these races that normally vary anywhere from 1-3 days requires months of conditioning and biking training. It's important to develop your body, capability and tolerance to cycle for prolonged time periods prior to being prepared to take part in the real race. This is where biking takes on a various significance for a lot of individuals as they end up being nearly addicted to the manner in which it makes them feel and yearn for the rush they receive from setting out on another biking course.

It's not to state that everyone gets involved in biking similarly, however, there is certainly a larger draw to the sport because of numerous competitive occasions rising up. This is terrific for the non- profits that have actually cash raised for them and outstanding for the people who get in shape and get drawn into such a gratifying sport. It's actually not surprising that as someone trains for a competitive race; they are rapidly pulled into the world of biking and all it can provide. This has actually really developed into a phenomenon and the bright side is that biking demonstrates no indications of slowing down anytime in the near future.

Cycling Can Involve the Family

There is a major epidemic of youth weight problems taking place in this nation, and for that reason, families have to determine methods to get and remain fit. As numerous households attempt to think about appealing methods to get fit together, they frequently rely on biking. This is an outstanding method to get in shape, burn some calories, and delight in some household bonding time. So for those households looking for a family activity that is going to enable them more time with one another and even enable them to get in shape, biking is the way to go.

Moms and dads desire the very best for their kids, and when they see that their kids are obese or dissatisfied, they rapidly recognize that it's time to do something. The issue with numerous kinds of workouts out there is that they feel like working out, and for that reason, kids will not stay with it.

Cycling, nevertheless, is something simple to enter into, fascinating, and provides an outstanding chance to bond with the family as you get fit. This is really a win-win for lots of moms and dads as they get to devote some time with their kids and enable them to get in shape while doing so. For the majority of kids, biking does not seem like an enormous endeavor or a workout program, it is rather something to eagerly anticipate as an activity to do with mother and father.

Biking can begin rather easily as simply a spin around the hood and even around the block. The secret to getting kids involved in any activity is to begin gradually to ensure that they do not get irritated or bored.

Biking can begin gradually and be developed to providing kids some excellent goal-setting capability as they develop their capability and endurance. When the household generally starts to get in much better shape, then it's time to step it up and discover some enjoyable courses and paths for the household.

Biking can rapidly end up being something to anticipate whenever time allows, as each time out is a brand-new experience. The kids can get included into choosing the areas or courses that the household sets out on. You rapidly see how biking can be an outstanding household bonding activity, however, one where the whole household gets in shape without ever seeming like they are working out.

Biking is Excellent for Getting in Shape

Individuals never ever used to look to an activity like biking as a robust physical fitness routine, however, times have actually changed. Those who used to believe that biking was simply a leisurely activity have a lot to discover as this could be among the most effective and extreme techniques of working out. If you're searching for a great exercise, then look no more as biking is going to assist to get you lean and fit rather rapidly-- it can work marvels when compared to other easier workouts that you might carry out in the gym.

Biking as an exceptional kind of workout is certainly something worth taking a look at, however, you simply have to log the miles to make it impactful. You get an incredible lower body exercise, along with pulling in the use of your chest, arms, and back as you bike your way to a much better body. This is among those workouts that draws in every element of your body to move you forward, which is what makes it among the most effective and thorough exercises out there.

In case you log the required miles through biking, you are going to see the weight actually disappear. You are going to then see your body beginning to get toned as you accumulate muscle in all the appropriate locations. You are going to see the most instant improvements in your legs and lower body in general as these are the muscles working the hardest in biking. If you seek a toned body, then this is the method to go without a doubt. When it concerns biking, however, you have to be sure that you develop gradually to stay clear of injury.

Biking could be rigorous and stressful, however well worth it in the long run. You are going to feel as if you can just go short distances in the beginning, however, it's actually clever to develop your endurance in time. Biking can assist you to look much better, and, to feel much better and definitely is going to build self-confidence at the same time. So if you have actually been having a hard time discovering an outstanding way of exercising, however, could not quite enter into something, then look no more. For lots of people, biking is among the most reliable and thorough exercises out there.

Biking for Health

Numerous people are having problems with weight or health conditions in some capability, and something actually has to be done. So when it boils down to getting in shape, individuals turn to workouts and sports that they feel comfy with. This is where biking can be found in as individuals seek this sport as a simple kind of workout. The majority of people can gain from getting much healthier and this can add to living a longer life that is far more satisfying. As individuals begin to understand that, they wish to discover something that is going to help them to rapidly get in shape and still take pleasure in the activity while they are making it happen.

Biking for health is a really familiar concept. If you consider it, a lot of us devoted several years of our youth on bikes, so the idea is rather comfy and familiar. This is among those workouts that does not constantly seem like a workout, though you do have to make a dedication to see the results. They state that the two finest methods to get yourself in much better shape is with appropriate diet plan and routine workout. One without the other does not work, therefore, in addition to the healthy eating comes the requirement to work out. This is why many individuals look to biking as their selected kind of getting fit.

Biking can assist you to burn significant calories, however in a moderate manner that does not ruin your body. Individuals of all walks of life and ages can delight in biking which's what makes it so attractive. You can discover some outstanding routes outdoors to practice your biking abilities, and if the weather condition turns bad, you can discover some exceptional choices inside your home too. Biking is extremely approachable, therefore, for those who want to acquire much better health, they rely on this as a beginning point.

You can cycle with others or by yourself as it is among those activities that work for practically any circumstance. If you're searching for an amazing kind of workout or have a vested interest in getting much healthier for any variety of reasons, then biking might simply be the activity that you have actually been trying to find. Even if you have not been on a bike for many years, biking can provide a gentle path into the realm of exercise and get you feeling much better practically instantly.

Biking to Improve Cardio

Biking is going to enhance heart muscles and is likewise considered an exceptional cardiovascular workout. Prior to starting any workout program, talk to your physician. Biking is a low impact workout that a person can take pleasure in throughout their lifetime.

Cardiovascular disease can consist of:

Coronary artery disease

Aorta disease Vascular disease

Pericardial disease

Heart valve disease

Heart failure

Abnormal heart rhythms

Congenital heart disease

Prevention:

Quit cigarette smoking

Lower cholesterol

Control high blood pressure

Work out

The benefits of an excellent cardio exercise are that it develops your stamina and even boosts your lung capability. Endorphins are launched and are going to offer you a natural high. You ought to raise your heart rate for 20 minutes, break out into a sweat. Energetic workout for 45 minutes every other day is going to be good for your heart.

Working out is likewise a stress reducer and all of us understand that tension impacts your heart. There is a link between heart problems and tension. You are going to constantly have some kind of stress, however, the technique is to manage it and not let it manage you. When your stress level increases, adrenaline boosts your heart rate and spikes up your blood pressure. Cortisol is a stress hormonal agent that is additionally launched and boosts sugars in the bloodstream. This, consequently, impacts your reproductive system, immune system, and digestion.

If you do not wish to cycle outside, you can register for a spinning class at your regional fitness center or purchase a stationary bicycle. The very best thing to do is attempt a spinning class initially to see if it is something that you wish to do prior to buying any tools.

If you wish to ride outdoors, then you ought to think about visiting your neighborhood bike store and getting a bike that is appropriate for you. You desire it to be simple and comfy to manage. Some kinds of bikes to select from, depending upon what you are going to be doing are exploring bikes, recumbent bikes, mtb, downhill bikes and those that are suitable for wheelchair racing.

Biking is not just an enjoyable sport to have, however, is likewise stress alleviating and heart-healthy. There are a lot of advantages that include biking. You can include your entire household or go solo. You can ride through the countryside and delight in the sounds.

Best Cycling Cities

Whether you bike sometimes for enjoyment or take pleasure in it often, it is excellent to understand which are the very best cities to bike in. Possibly you have a buddy who resides in one, and you have to understand if you ought to bring your bike when you visit. Or, there might be a town near you, or perhaps the one you reside in, that you simply need to explore.

Portland, Oregon, is frequently pointed out as the very best cycling city in the USA. With rivers, forests, mountains, and other natural marvels around, it is no surprise. Portland is a bike-friendly city with bike lanes on numerous huge roadways, and even some unique roadways only for bikes. If you wish to commute to work here, it is really simple. Or, if you choose, it is a terrific location to take a leisurely trip.

Minneapolis, Minnesota, might be unexpected to some. Nevertheless, when it is not snowing, it is an excellent location to bike. This twin city is really enjoyable to check out, and an ideal location to bring a bike. Seattle, Washington, is another exceptional location. With the Puget Noise simply close by, you make certain to get an exceptional view of a city hill. Even with the infamous northwest damp weather, cycling in the fresh air of Seattle is difficult to beat.

San Francisco, California, is among the most special locations in California. What could beat a great view of the stunning Golden Gate Bridge, or cycling down the windiest roadway on the planet? With amazing and brand-new things to see on each street, it is no surprise San Francisco made the list.

Madison, Wisconsin, is a really bike-friendly city, and this does not appear to be altering. In Madison, you can bike around the city or around a lake. The bike paths are easy for even unskilled cyclists to utilize.

Austin, Texas, is frequently compared to Portland, and it is simple to see why. Both of these fantastic cities are on the list of the very best locations to bike. Austin is bike-friendly, and there are numerous things to see. You get the advantages of a location such as Portland without the pesky northwest rain. Naturally, there are a lot more fantastic cities to bike. As a matter of fact, you might take advantage of almost any city.

Excellent Bike Trails

Whether you are a beginner cyclist or a skilled one, you have to understand where the terrific bike routes are. Even though you can not visit and ride them all, it is possible you are going to have the ability to ride a few of them. The experience of the best bike routes are great, and cyclists of all capabilities are going to enjoy them.

In each and every single state, there are bike routes that are ideal for biking. Some remain in city locations, others remain in backwoods. There are a lot of bike routes that have actually been transformed from railroad tracks. Some routes are paved, others are grass or dirt. Regardless of where you live, there are bound to be fantastic bike tracks someplace close by, or in your state. The Okanogan Area of Washington state is on lots of lists as one of the very best cycling routes around. In northern Washington, in between Seattle and Spokane, is this excellent location to bike. Wonderful views, fresh air and wildlife sightings await.

The driftless part of Wisconsin remains in the southern part of the state. This part of the state has valleys and hills that are really enjoyable to ride in. If you are a beginner rider, it might be best to wait up until you have a greater level of proficiency. The downs and ups of riding in this area can make for a difficult trip.

Cajun County in Louisiana, provides some wonderful panoramas. Surrounding the Gulf of Mexico, there are additionally bayous, swamps and more for your watching and riding satisfaction. It can get quite hot, so take care. Sugarloaf Moutain in the state of Maryland is a terrific location to ride for clean air, wildlife sightings, views, and a cool breeze. An included advantage is the reasonably close distance to Washington, D.C.

Lastly, Acadia National Park in Maine, has actually long been a destination for cyclists.

There are numerous routes, over one hundred miles worth, that it appears difficult to see all the things. This national forest permits outdoor camping, so it might be best to remain there for a night and get the complete experience. Wherever you live, there are excellent locations to ride your bike simply waiting to be discovered. Even if your state is not recognized for being bike-friendly, you simply need to try to find locations to ride. Lots of trekking tracks permit bikes, so think about looking into hiking tracks if you can not discover lots of cycling tracks. Simply make certain to verify that bikes are enabled.

Cycling to Work

Cycling to work could be a tall order, even for the dedicated bicycle rider. With altering weather, time restraints, and more, it is a difficult dedication to make. The very best method to begin cycling to work is to do so gradually. Possibly begin with one day weekly, and after that, slowly boost the frequency.

In some locations, it simply is not practical to bike to work year-round. Nevertheless, you definitely can bike to work throughout the spring, summer season, and part of fall in many areas. If you reside in a more southern state, you might have the ability to bike to work all year long.

Cycling to work is going to spare you cash on gas, which is among the more apparent advantages. Nevertheless, it is going to additionally spare you stress given that you do not need to be in traffic and be worried. Additionally, you are going to be getting a good deal of activity that you generally do not get. Even if your work is a mile from your home, if you bike to and from work everyday, that is 10 miles of cycling that you would not have actually had every week. Not just that, however, cycling, rather than driving, aids the environment, since the exhaust from your vehicle is not creating contamination.

There are numerous things you may do to enhance your health, and cycling to work is a fantastic method to begin. The workout you get while riding your bike to work is really excellent. There are a couple of other methods to get as much activity and contribute a lot to your health daily. Besides, the majority of people do not have an hour or 2 every day for the fitness center. Rather, include some time to your commute, and exercise on your way to work.

It is simple to obtain a bag or a storage basket for your bike, so you can bring a change of clothing with you on your bike, and even a brief-case or knapsack. In this manner, if you get unclean or sweat a bit while riding your bike to work, you can still appear competent and clean-cut when you show up, as quickly as you change. There are lots of methods to cycle, and cycling to work is simply one method to begin. It is simple to attempt, and lots of people live sufficiently close to their location of work to try it.

Travel Trips

Biking is among those sports that you can get to know when you are little and continue well into your golden years. Actually, you can cycle forever. Do you recall when you got your initial bike? Recall the enjoyment when you could ride without the training wheels? The adventure of understanding that you can brake and remain upright is one memory that you might always remember.

Among the very best aspects of biking is that you may do it with your buddies or alone. You can ride close to the lakes, oceans and rivers. There are groups that are going to take you along back roads to view the countryside that you would otherwise simply go by if you remained in a vehicle. There are cycling tracks in lots of parts of the nation now where you can ride through cities in addition to the countryside. You can likewise schedule a cycling journey through lots of nations and experience special cultures.

When you are selecting a trip, think about if you wish to go on your own or with a directed trip. Directed trips could be enjoyable and more secure for you if you are not of a daring spirit. The drawback of it is that you are going to need to follow them and not have the ability to take side trips. Each has its bad and good, so decide based upon what you are at ease doing. Utilize your favorite online search engine to discover travel alternatives. Some are environmentally friendly and consist of the choice of biking and walking, which may be something you would have an interest in.

When you choose where you wish to go, take note of a few of these rules of the road:

Earphones ought to not be used while biking

Fill medical prescriptions

Purchase an additional set of contacts or glasses

Make certain you understand all of your tools

Bring a notable credit card and/or traveler's checks

Pay your expenses prior to leaving

Leave a copy of your travel plan with a relied on buddy or member of the family.

Above all, ensure you train well prior to leaving, however, do not overtrain so much that you are too exhausted to take pleasure in the trip. Preserve a level of training that is going to be constant with the geographical location where you are going to be riding. Ask others who have actually done this for their ideas.

Cycling Events

If you have an interest in biking, and taking advantage of biking, you need to check out cycling events. Biking could be biking for others or for yourself, and it is a terrific method to enrich the world around you. You can assist the environment, your health, and even raise money and awareness for other people.

Lots of cycling events are charitable events, so you can feel excellent about having fun and cycling. These cycling events can generate income for a charitable company in a variety of methods. Initially, they typically charge an admittance charge to riders. For instance, you might need to pay twenty dollars, however, that cash is contributed to the company the trip is for. Or, you might have to acquire sponsors who are going to donate to the organization.

Usually, these cycling events are fairly long, and frequently have stops for bathrooms and resting. Sometimes, they are going to likewise have actually gotten corporate sponsorships and are going to give out beverages such as energy beverages, water, or energy bars. These donated things are free of charge to riders. Due to this, the majority of the time you are going to get back in items the cash you paid to ride, to begin with, depending upon the quantity. Cycling events such as these are comparable in numerous methods to marathons, other than the fact that you are on a bike rather than walking or running. The length of cycling events differ substantially, depending upon the objective of the event and the path.

There are likewise lots of cycling events that are not for charity, however, they are just for enjoyment. Depending upon where you live, there might be cycling events to check out the city, like riding throughout all the regional bridges or riding down and up a regional mountain. Many huge cities provide a great deal of cycling events, and with a little bit of research, you can discover the ones that intrigue you.

The more you bike, the much better it is for your health, and the more you are enhancing yourself. Not just that, however, you are motivating those around you and those who see you riding to ride themselves, which can have a big ecological effect. Leading by example, simply put, is a proven method to cycle. And riding in a cycling event is a terrific method to take advantage of biking.

Organized Bike Rides

A growing number of individuals today have an interest in enhancing their lives with biking. Cycling to work, to the shop, or only for workout and fresh air are exceptionally typical. Cycling is likewise a fantastic method to meet brand-new individuals and find things in your location you never ever understood existed.

A fast web search can assist you to discover neighborhood bicycle riders who are attempting to get in touch with others. If you discover a group that bikes together, see about joining them. There are frequently numerous groups that arrange big bike flights and welcome new members. Generally, these groups are cost-free. It is most likely that you are going to have the ability to discover rides that suit your physical capabilities. If you are a fairly brand-new rider, try to find something that is short and not too exhausting. The majority of groups have a great deal of trips, and you do not need to take part in them all.

Riding with a group can likewise be more secure than riding alone, since your group of cyclists is going to be really noticeable. Signing up with an arranged bike trip is going to be exciting, enjoyable and might even be an academic experience. If you are brand-new to a location, or simply brand-new to cycling in a location, you are going to definitely find all sorts of brand-new things. It is possible that there are all sorts of cool things in your location you have actually never ever seen prior. On a bike, you can go to a lot more locations than in vehicles.

If the arranged bike trip is big enough, it is possible that some streets are going to even be closed down, increasing your security exceptionally. This is not quite typical for daily trips, but for huge riding occasions, it takes place constantly.

If you like to ride your bike, you simply need to take advantage of biking with arranged bike trips. All you need to do is appear and ride, so it is a lot easier than planning a path out on your own. Not just that, however you can also meet other riders who delight in riding, so you understand you are going to have a thing in common with them.

Depending upon the length of your arranged bike trip, there might be breaks worked into the routine. This is going to provide you time to rest, eat and utilize the restroom, as required. Lots of arranged bike trips are simply around a local area for an hour or 2, and others are of a longer range and possibly even overnight. Make certain to choose an arranged trip that you fccl comfy with.

The Biking Getaway

Many individuals are trying to find alternative holiday types nowadays. Either due to hard monetary times or the need for a more imaginative kind of vacation, individuals are trying to find options that can provide enjoyment and a more affordable choice. This has to do with the fact that lots of people rely on biking as a getaway alternative. The charm of a biking holiday is that it includes some terrific exercise and likewise a method of having a look at the surroundings in the locations you check out. Biking provides all the different elements of what individuals search for in a getaway, and for that reason, has actually ended up being an incredibly popular activity to focus a getaway around.

A biking holiday can occur anywhere. It could be on a camping area, at a national forest, or as part of a larger holiday. All it takes is a bike and some determination to take a look at the neighborhood landscapes and take in some brand-new tracks. This is enticing for the person or household who wishes to remain healthy even on holiday, or for those that want to see every inch of the location they take a trip to. Biking is a friendly activity as it interests individuals of every age, and for that reason, that makes it enjoyable and friendly. There are even some locations out there that allow no motorized vehicles within their borders, permitting just bikes. This is the ideal place for those that wish to have a look at the charm of nature and return to a more simplified lifestyle. This is the basis of a terrific biking holiday.

Biking as a holiday choice never ever used to be rather so prominent, however, the sport has actually acquired some significant attention recently. Couple the boost in the appeal of this sport with the truth that individuals have to take more affordable holidays in difficult financial times and you discover that a biking holiday is really a slam dunk for everybody. If you want to take a more daring path for your holiday requirements, and you wish to get fit in the procedure, then this is absolutely an outstanding choice. If you have actually never ever thought about a biking holiday, then now might be the time. You can discover some fantastic tracks, locations, and go to some truly terrific locations at the same time.

There are Options for All Ages

Today, individuals are working out at almost any age. While the older one gets, the options might seem restricting. One exercise choice for individuals of any age is cycling. As a matter of fact, biking is a choice that numerous individuals entering their senior years have actually picked for keeping fit. Say you have actually gotten to your 4th decade and even higher. You aren't as fit as you used to be, however, you still wish to work up a great sweat and feel in control of things. There are still a number of choices for a workout. Amongst them are running, swimming, low-impact aerobics, and, yes, cycling. For the 40-year-old, or older, for instance, cycling ends up being an excellent workout choice, specifically for individuals with osteoarthritis of the knees. And the very best solution for a knee issue might be a stationary bicycle.

The bright side is that stationary bicycles can be found in lots of shapes. For instance, there's an upright stationary bicycle. It's maybe the most typical stationary bicycle that comes to your mind. It looks like a street bike. The good idea about uprights is that they do not need much area. They feel extremely natural, particularly to the bicycle rider who truly wants to be out on the road. Additionally, some upright bike exercisers declare that they get a much better exercise than riding on the street. That's due to the fact that on a stationary bicycle, there is more effort put into the experience.

Another stationary bicycle choice is the recumbent stationary bicycle. It's specifically useful for individuals with back or balance issues. These bikes likewise provide more cushioning. In a lot of cases, recumbent stationary bicycles might be much easier to ride. While comparing stationary bicycles, do not ignore the dual-action fixed machine. It integrates upright workout with movable handlebars. This choice offers the rider's arms a genuine workout. While numerous stationary bicycles provide lower-body workouts, the dual-action bike provides much better comprehensive overall fitness. Generally, these bikes cost more and are typically bigger than other stationary bicycles.

So, if biking is your thing, however, age is a barrier, a stationary bicycle might be the solution. Exercises on stationary bicycles are low-impact; yet make it possible for the bicycle rider to burn a great deal of calories. Maybe the very best function of a stationary bicycle is that the opportunities of striking an unanticipated mud puddle are slim to none.

The Health Advantages of Biking

There are numerous health advantages to biking, it is practically inconceivable to recount them all. As such, just a few are going to be checked out. Everybody understands that cycling is a fantastic method to enhance health, however, it is essential to understand simply how great cycling is for you.

Cycling is among the very best kinds of workout, for a variety of reasons. Initially, for many individuals, it is much easier to burn calories on a bike than doing another activity. The reason for this differs from one person to another, however, many individuals believe that it is since cycling is so enjoyable. Likewise, it is simple to do. There is even a statement about how individuals always remember how to ride a bike. Even if you have not ridden a bike in years, odds are you still understand how.

A terrific health advantage of biking is that your metabolic process is going to increase. Working out, in general, jump-starts your metabolic process, permitting you to burn more calories and fat. With an increased metabolic process, it is going to be much easier for you to reach any health objectives you might have, and even a target weight if you wish to shed pounds.

With a greater metabolic process and routine workout on your bike, you are going to begin to burn fat. Even if you do not always wish to reduce weight, burning fat is great. Many people have a greater portion of body fat than they ought to, and burning that fat assists to keep you healthier. While burning fat on your bike, you are going to likewise be growing muscle. Riding a bike is an activity that uses mainly your lower body, however, it does work your core and your upper body a little also. Building muscle is going to offer you a healthy appearance, you are going to feel much better, and be more powerful.

Cycling likewise assists you to maintain your stamina or endurance, particularly when you bike as a cardiovascular endeavor. It is essential for your total health that you boost your heart rate while working out. While you might not wish to bike quickly for your whole trip, maybe doing so for a mile or more is going to be a huge aid to your health.

Lastly, working out has actually been stated to boost your total level of joy. Naturally, getting fresh air while you opt for a trip makes sure to raise your state of mind anyhow. With both psychological and physical advantages, biking looks like an excellent option.

The Ecological Advantages of Biking

If you are thinking about ending up being a bicycle rider, or if you currently are a bicycle rider, you understand there are a variety of advantages to biking for life. You can enhance your own health, the health of those around you by leading by example, and even the world around you by assisting the environment. While assisting the environment can appear like a huge job, it is possible to have a positive impact with little actions. Biking is simply another thing you can do to make sure the world ends up being a much better, healthier location.

When you bike rather than drive in your daily life, you do a lot of good for the environment around you. For instance, you are assisting to reduce the commotion level on your commuting path. If your car is not taking its regular path, it is not making sounds. This reduced noise level assists the locations you drive through and around to end up being more habitable areas.

While it might appear as if simply one vehicle lacking from your commute path is going to make a distinction, the truth is that it is going to.

You might not observe, however, it does have an effect. While inspiring others to bike like you do, you are going to be reducing the noise level a lot more. Obviously, among the most apparent ecological advantages of biking is pollution. Even vehicles that boast excellent gas mileage release contamination in their exhaust. If you bike rather than driving, you are assisting to reduce vehicle emissions, which assists with less greenhouse gases. Maybe you do not wish to bike to work every day. If you bike to work even one day a week or month, your actions are going to have terrific effects. If each and every single individual biked to work only one day a week or month, the ecological advantages would be nearly inconceivable.

Lastly, leading by example is an ecological advantage of biking. If you influence even a single person to bike sometimes rather than driving, you are affecting pollution and noise levels a lot more. Even if you do not persuade somebody outright to bike, someone might see you riding past them on your path to work every day, which is going to assist to persuade them to do the identical thing.

I hope that you enjoyed reading through this book and that you have found it useful. If you want to share your thoughts on this book, you can do so by leaving a review on the Amazon page. Have a great rest of the day.

Printed in Great Britain
by Amazon